Mind the Load

How to Stop Carrying It All and Start Sharing the Mental Workload

Written by
LYLA HARRINGTON

© **Copyright LEH Publishing 2025 - All rights reserved.**

The content within this book may not be reproduced, duplicated or transmitted without direct written permission from the author or the publisher.

Under no circumstances will any blame or legal responsibility be held against the publisher, or author, for any damages, reparation, or monetary loss due to the information contained within this book. Either directly or indirectly. You are responsible for your own choices, actions, and results.

Legal Notice:

This book is copyright protected. This book is only for personal use. You cannot amend, distribute, sell, use, quote or paraphrase any part, of the content within this book, without the consent of the author or publisher.

Disclaimer Notice:

Please note the information contained within this document is for educational and entertainment purposes only. All effort has been expended to present accurate, up-to-date, and reliable, complete information. No warranties of any kind are declared or implied. Readers acknowledge that the author is not engaging in the rendering of legal, financial, medical or professional advice. The content within this book has been derived from various sources. Please consult a licensed professional before attempting any techniques outlined in this book.

By reading this document, the reader agrees that under no circumstances is the author responsible for any losses, direct or indirect, which are incurred as a result of the use of the information contained within this document, including, but not limited to, — errors, omissions, or inaccuracies.

ISBN: 978-1-7638678-4-0

Table of Contents

Introduction 4
Chapter 1 10
    Understanding the Mental Load
Chapter 2 18
    The Impact of the Mental Load
Chapter 3 26
    Communication and Conflict Resolution
Chapter 4 34
    Strategies for Equitable Task Distribution
Chapter 5 41
    Emotional and Cognitive Load Management   41
Chapter 6 50
    Overcoming Obstacles and Objections
Chapter 7 59
    Exercises and Tools for Change
Chapter 8 67
    Real Couples, Real Solutions: Stories of Change
Chapter 9 77
    Sustaining Long-Term Change
Conclusion 84
    Household Audit: A Comprehensive Task List   89

Introduction

Imagine this: it's 9 p.m. The kids are finally asleep after what felt like an Olympic triathlon of bath time, bedtime stories, and last-minute homework crises. You finally sit down, ready to revel in the sweet silence, but your mind has other plans. It catapults ahead, assembling tomorrow's to-do list at lightning speed—what needs packing for lunch, which uniform needs washing, and whether there's enough petrol in the car to make it to soccer practice. Meanwhile, the dishwasher hums its judgment in the background, and your partner, blissfully unaware of your mental marathon, casually asks, "Did you remember to pay the electricity bill?"

You stare at the calendar, a chaotic masterpiece of colour-coded reminders: work deadlines, school events, your own doctor's appointment that you rescheduled—again. Somewhere between realizing you've run out of milk and debating whether you have the willpower to fold the Everest of laundry in the corner, it dawns on you—this isn't just about being busy. It's about carrying it all: the invisible responsibilities, the relentless to-do list, and the exhausting task of being the family's all-knowing, all-planning mastermind.

Meanwhile, your partner, well-meaning but blissfully unaware, lounges on the couch, scrolling through their phone, seemingly convinced that their single contribution of 'helping with the dishes' somehow balances out the endless to-do list running through your head.

This, my friends, is the mental load. And it's absolutely exhausting.

I'm writing this book as a full-time working mum of three who has spent years juggling the demands of family, career, and, let's be honest, the unrealistic expectation of having it all together. Society constantly reinforces these expectations, with media glorifying the image of the "supermum" who balances everything flawlessly and cultural norms suggesting that women are naturally better at managing households. These pressures leave many of us feeling inadequate when we fall short, even though the expectations themselves are unreasonable. It's a cycle that's exhausting and unsustainable, but one we can begin to break by naming and addressing it.

There was a moment, not too long ago, when I found myself sitting in my car in the grocery store parking lot, cursing the gods because I had forgotten my youngest had to bring in cupcakes the next day for a class party, and heaven help me if they weren't gluten-free, egg-free, dairy-free, and blessed by an organic, ethically sourced unicorn. But in that moment, I decided to reclaim my sanity—I walked straight to the bakery, grabbed the most sugar-laden, allergen-filled cupcakes I could find, and marched to the checkout like a warrior who had chosen chaos. And you know what? The kids survived. In fact, they loved them. And I lived to see another day, realizing that sometimes, good enough is truly good enough. That moment made me realize I needed to start sharing the mental load more openly—so I called my partner, handed over some responsibilities, and finally let go of the idea that I had to manage everything alone. It wasn't the forgotten cupcakes that broke me—it was the realization that I was constantly running on empty, managing everyone else's needs while barely keeping up with my own. If you've ever felt like the household CEO, emotional manager, and scheduling maestro all rolled into one, this book is for you.

The mental load isn't just about physical tasks; it's about the cognitive and emotional labour that goes into keeping everything running smoothly. This includes remembering every family member's appointments, planning meals that accommodate dietary preferences, ensuring school forms are submitted on time, and anticipating emotional needs—whether it's comforting a child after a tough day or knowing when your partner needs extra support. These responsibilities are often invisible but crucial, requiring constant mental energy and emotional investment. It's the kind of work that often goes unnoticed but is absolutely vital. It's exhausting, yet many of us bear this load silently, thinking it's just part of being a partner, a parent, or an adult. But here's the thing: it doesn't have to be this way. Through this book, my goal is to shine a light on the mental load, break down its impact on our lives and relationships, and offer practical strategies to lighten the burden.

Over the coming chapters, we'll unpack what the mental load really means and why it's so pervasive. We'll delve into its historical roots, how it manifests in modern relationships, and the emotional and cognitive toll it takes. You'll explore practical strategies for equitable task distribution, tips for improving communication, and tools for managing emotional labour. Each chapter will guide you through these themes with relatable examples and actionable insights, offering a roadmap to create more balance and harmony in your life.

We'll talk about those unspoken frustrations when tasks aren't divided fairly, the silent resentment that creeps in, and the moments of burnout that leave us questioning how we got here. You'll find relatable anecdotes, research-backed insights, and actionable steps to help you create a more balanced and equitable approach to managing life's responsibilities. Whether you're looking to improve communication with your partner, set boundaries, or simply find ways to reclaim your time and energy, this book has something for you.

The mental load isn't just a personal issue—it's a societal one. Deeply ingrained cultural norms often perpetuate the expectation that women should take the lead in managing household and emotional responsibilities. For instance, even in dual-income households, studies consistently show that women shoulder the majority of childcare planning, meal coordination, and household management. These norms are reinforced by media portrayals of women as natural multitaskers and caregivers, leaving little room for equitable sharing of responsibilities.

By challenging these expectations, we can begin to redefine what fairness looks like in modern relationships. When we address it, we not only improve our individual well-being but also strengthen our relationships and set a better example for the next generation. Tackling the mental load is about creating a culture that values equity and shared responsibility. It's about teaching our children—particularly girls—that household and emotional labour should never fall solely on one person. It's about pushing back against the outdated norms that expect women to be the default managers of everything home and family-related.

By the time you turn the last page, I want you to feel empowered with the tools and insights to bring more balance into your life. Change doesn't happen overnight, and progress may be gradual, but even small steps can make a significant difference. Whether it's delegating a single task, setting boundaries for the first time, or simply acknowledging the weight of the mental load, every action contributes to long-term transformation. The key is consistency and patience—over time, these efforts will add up to meaningful change. Small changes can lead to big transformations, and together, we can start making those changes today.

This isn't just a book; it's a conversation—one that encourages you to reflect on your own experiences, connect with others, and find strategies that work for your unique situation. Along the way, you'll encounter stories from people just like you who have found ways to shift their mental load and reclaim their lives. Their journeys will remind you that change is possible, even when it feels daunting.

So, grab a cup of tea (or let's be real, maybe a glass of wine), get comfortable, and let's dive in. Together, we'll uncover the strategies and tools you need to take control of your mental load and create a life that feels lighter, more balanced, and genuinely fulfilling. This is your invitation to step off the hamster wheel and take a breath. It's time to mind the load, and together, we're going to find a way forward—one manageable step at a time.

Chapter 1

Understanding the Mental Load

Let's start with a simple question: have you ever woken up in the middle of the night and immediately started ticking through your mental to-do list? From remembering to pack your child's lunch to booking a dentist appointment for your partner to noting that the dog's vaccinations are due next month—all while figuring out what's for dinner tomorrow. This, my friend, is the mental load. It's not the same as physically doing the chores, though you're probably doing those too. It's the constant mental juggling act of keeping everything in motion, and it's utterly invisible to anyone not carrying it. The weight of it doesn't just sit in your brain; it lingers in your shoulders, tightens your back, and sneaks into moments when you should be unwinding. Even when you finally sit down, your mind races ahead, planning, anticipating, and calculating, never truly switching off. You might notice it when you wake up with a stiff neck after a restless night of tossing and turning, or when a seemingly small task feels insurmountable because you're running on empty. It shows up in chronic stress, those nagging headaches that won't go away, and the tension that never quite leaves your body, even during a weekend meant for rest. The physical toll is just as relentless as the mental one, making it impossible to fully unwind. It never truly goes away.

The mental load is like being the project manager of your household—except there's no pay, no perks, and the stakeholders (your family) are notoriously difficult to manage and, dare I say it, a little ungrateful. Imagine running a never-ending meeting in your head: keeping tabs on everyone's needs while feeling the weight of every task that hasn't yet been done. It's not just the tasks themselves but the emotional exhaustion of constantly anticipating, planning, and preventing potential disasters. The sheer effort it takes to stay one step ahead leaves little room to breathe, let alone feel appreciated for all the work that goes unnoticed. It's the weight of being the one who not only remembers that someone needs new shoes but also figures out when to buy them, what size, and how to fit the shopping trip into an already packed schedule without causing a meltdown—either theirs or yours. It's making sure the pantry is stocked, the birthday gifts are wrapped, and the extracurricular activities don't overlap. It's exhausting, unrelenting, and often completely thankless. Yet, for many of us, it's just "what we do." And the irony? Often, no one notices—until something doesn't get done.

One day, I was at a friend's barbecue, listening to her recount how her husband "helped" by loading the dishwasher. "He asked me if he was doing it right," she said, rolling her eyes. "Meanwhile, I'm the one who's figured out how to fit in the baking sheets, chopsticks, and sippy cups while planning next week's meals in my head." Her frustration struck a chord. It wasn't just about the dishwasher; it was about the invisible burden of always having to know, plan, and manage. This story is so universal it could have come from any one of us. We've all had those moments of exasperation when the so-called help feels more like another task to supervise.

But let's zoom out for a moment. The mental load isn't just about who does what; it's about the emotional toll of always being "the one." It's about those moments of resentment when you realise your partner didn't even notice that the toothpaste was running low or that your child's school form was due last week. It's about the silent frustration of always having to ask for help because no one else sees what needs to be done. Imagine this: you notice the overflowing trash bin and decide to leave it, wondering how long it will take before someone else takes responsibility. Days go by, and the bin remains untouched, growing into a symbol of neglect. Eventually, you take it out, but the act feels less like a chore and more like a confirmation that no one else is paying attention. This dynamic breeds resentment, as the person carrying the load begins to feel not only unseen but also unvalued in their efforts to keep everything running smoothly. It's about burnout—pure and simple. And burnout isn't just feeling tired; it's a chronic state of emotional, physical, and mental exhaustion that leaves you wondering how you're supposed to keep going. The toll isn't just on you—it's on your relationships, your health, and your happiness.

The key to managing this load is awareness. Recognizing the mental load is the first step in addressing it. It's about fostering open communication with your partner, making the invisible visible, and getting everyone on the same page. Initiating discussions about who does what and when can transform your relationship dynamics. When you both see the full picture, you can start redistributing tasks in a way that feels fair and manageable.

To understand how we ended up with the mental load as a household staple, we need to rewind the clock a bit. Picture this: it's the mid-20th century, and society is a little obsessed with its idea of gender roles. Men were the breadwinners, carrying briefcases to work, while women were the homemakers, armed with aprons and a vacuum cleaner. This division of labor was clear-cut, but it didn't account for the emotional and cognitive tasks women took on, like remembering birthdays and managing kids' tantrums. These roles were rooted in the belief that each gender had distinct, non-overlapping spheres of responsibility. But as history would have it, things started to change. Economic shifts, like the Industrial Revolution, began pulling more women into the workforce. The rigid Victorian gender roles began to wobble, setting the stage for a new era.

Enter the feminist movements of the 1960s and 70s, which were less of a gentle wave and more of a seismic shift in societal norms. Women demanded more than just a paycheck; they wanted equality in every aspect of life, including at home. These movements challenged the status quo, pushing for partnerships where both parties shared the load, be it financial or domestic. No longer were women expected to bear the brunt of household management unaided. The idea was simple yet revolutionary: both partners should contribute equally, not just to the family income, but to the family life. This push for equitable partnerships started to change what was expected from men and women, allowing them to step into roles traditionally reserved for the other gender. Feminism opened the door for conversations about the mental load long before the term was coined.

Fast forward to today, and the landscape of relationships looks quite different. With more women in the workforce than ever before, many households are now dual-income. This shift means that traditional roles have become blurred, and responsibilities at home are increasingly shared. Gone are the days when one partner was solely responsible for the upkeep of the household while the other focused on earning a living. Now, it's all about teamwork. However, despite these changes, the mental load hasn't vanished; it's just taken on new forms. Couples are navigating this shared space, trying to strike a balance between career and home life. It's a dance, and sometimes we all step on each other's toes.

This isn't just a women's issue, though. The mental load exists in all types of relationships. Same-sex couples, childfree partnerships, and even roommates share versions of this invisible burden. A friend once told me about her roommate who seemed oblivious to the fact that clean towels didn't magically reappear in the bathroom. She joked about instituting a chore chart but felt like even managing that would end up on her plate. Whether you're married with kids or sharing a flat with friends, someone usually ends up being the "manager"—and if it's you, it can feel isolating and unfair. It's not about who takes out the trash; it's about who's always expected to notice when it's full.

While past generations often accepted traditional gender roles without question, today's shifting dynamics are challenging those norms. In some families, these expectations are being redefined, with partners actively working toward more equitable divisions of labor. Others, however, still grapple with ingrained beliefs that one person should carry the bulk of household responsibilities. The mental load doesn't just pass from one person to another—it evolves, shaped by societal expectations, economic pressures, and generational shifts. Recognizing these changes helps us understand not only where we are now but also how we can push for a more balanced future.

When we talk about the mental load, it's easy to picture a harried mom juggling kids, work, and a household. But the truth is, this isn't just a one-woman show or even a strictly heterosexual issue. Mental load affects everyone in relationships, regardless of gender or family setup. In same-sex partnerships, for instance, the division of tasks often looks different. Partners typically negotiate roles without the societal blueprint of traditional gender roles, which can lead to a more balanced distribution of responsibilities. They tend to approach the mental load with a sense of equity from the get-go, which can serve as a model for all of us. Then there are childfree couples, who, despite not having kids in the mix, still face an array of responsibilities that need managing—from who's in charge of keeping track of social engagements to ensuring the dog gets his heartworm pills on time. Even without the pitter-patter of little feet, the mental load is alive and well.

Stories from diverse relationship structures further illustrate this reality. Take non-binary individuals who may find themselves navigating roles not traditionally assigned by society. A non-binary person might take on what are considered "feminine" tasks in one relationship and "masculine" ones in another, depending on the dynamics at play. This fluidity can lead to a more personalized approach to managing mental load, one that doesn't rely on outdated stereotypes. Diverse family setups, like those with multiple generations under one roof or blended families, add another layer of complexity. Here, the mental load involves coordinating between various needs, schedules, and expectations, often requiring a higher degree of organization and communication. In these scenarios, everyone pitches in, yet the mental load may still fall disproportionately on one person, highlighting the need for ongoing dialogue about shared responsibilities.

But here's the real question: why does this matter? Because acknowledging the mental load is the first step to addressing it. When we talk about it, we make the invisible visible. We start to see the patterns in our relationships and recognise the need for change. This book isn't about assigning blame; it's about finding solutions. It's about building awareness, fostering empathy, and creating systems that work for everyone in the household. It's about learning how to share the load—not just in theory but in practice. By naming it, we can challenge the idea that it's just part of life and begin to reshape our expectations.

Exercise: The Household Audit

Ready to make the invisible visible? Take a moment to write down everything you do to keep your household running. Include tasks like scheduling appointments, planning meals, and keeping track of birthdays. Once you have your list, sit down with your partner and compare notes. Discuss which tasks you can share or delegate. This exercise is a great way to open the lines of communication and start the conversation about balancing the load.

By recognizing and addressing the mental load, you create a foundation for a more balanced and harmonious relationship. It's not about keeping score; it's about understanding and supporting each other in the way you both need.

If you're not sure where to start you can use our starter list of tasks located on page 89.

Chapter 2

The Impact of the Mental Load

It starts subtly. You feel more tired than usual, brushing it off as just another busy day. But then, day after day, the fatigue deepens. Tasks that once seemed routine now feel monumental, like climbing Everest in flip-flops. Emotional exhaustion doesn't announce itself with a neon sign; it creeps in like a fog, clouding your mind and weighing down your heart. If you've ever sat in your car, staring blankly at the dashboard after running errands, feeling utterly drained, you know exactly what I'm talking about.

Emotional burnout from the mental load isn't just about being physically tired—it's the chronic fatigue that seeps into your very core, affecting everything from how you make decisions to how you engage with daily life. Simple choices, like what to cook for dinner or which task to prioritise, become overwhelming. Even routine activities, like responding to emails or planning a family outing, can feel like monumental hurdles. This fatigue clouds your judgment, slows your reactions, and leaves you second-guessing yourself, as though the sheer act of thinking has become another item on an already overloaded to-do list. It's the emotional numbness that makes even joyful moments feel muted and the lack of motivation that has you scrolling endlessly on your phone instead of tackling your to-do list. It's not because you're lazy or ungrateful; it's because your reserves are empty. The endless multitasking, the constant vigilance, and the lack of appreciation for all that invisible work take their toll. And when these feelings compound over weeks, months, or even years, they begin to shape your sense of self-worth and capacity to cope.

As a working mum of three and a full-time teacher, I often feel like I'm on a hamster wheel, running as fast as I can but never getting anywhere. My days are a blur of early morning school prep for the kids, a full day of teaching, afternoon activities, and late-night lesson planning. Meanwhile, my husband, a consultant working long hours into the night, is often unavailable to share the household load during the week. At one point, I tried making detailed lists and delegating tasks to him, but even then, I found myself micromanaging the execution. It felt like more work to explain what needed to be done than to just do it myself.

My turning point came when a last-minute school deadline forced me to step back from managing everything at home. With no choice but to let things go, I realized that not everything required my constant oversight. I saw that my kids were capable of handling some responsibilities, and my husband, when given clear expectations, could step up and take on more without constant reminders. It was then that I realized how much of my mental energy was tied up in tasks that could be shared or even let go entirely.

Slowly, I began setting clearer boundaries and prioritising my own well-being, a shift that transformed not just my schedule but also my mindset. Between managing work deadlines, remembering my children's extra-curricular schedules, and keeping track of household supplies, I felt like there was no room left for myself. It's not just the tasks. It's the constant thinking about the tasks that wears me down. My story is not unique. For many, the mental load creates a cycle of constant planning and exhaustion, leaving little energy for joy or spontaneity. And when there's no time to recharge, burnout becomes inevitable.

This kind of emotional exhaustion doesn't just affect you; it seeps into your relationships too. Unevenly distributed tasks, unspoken frustrations, and unmet expectations create a perfect storm for relationship strain. Picture this: you've spent your day juggling work calls, meal prep, and homework duty. You're physically drained, your brain is buzzing with tomorrow's to-do list, and you're desperate for a moment to catch your breath. Your partner, mindlessly oblivious, comes home from work and asks, "What's for dinner?" Internally, you feel a pang of frustration, your mind racing with thoughts like, "Can't you see how much I've already done today?" and "Why is this always my problem to solve?" It's not the question itself that stings; it's the implication that everything—

planning, shopping, cooking—is your responsibility. Over time, these small moments of imbalance accumulate, driving a wedge of resentment and emotional distance between partners.

I once spoke with a couple, both busy professionals, who found themselves constantly arguing over what seemed like trivial issues. The root of their conflict? The unspoken expectations around who managed what. The wife felt overwhelmed by the mental load, while the husband, genuinely unaware, didn't realise the extent of her burden. "She'd snap at me for not cleaning the kitchen, but I didn't even notice it needed cleaning," he admitted. It wasn't until they sat down and openly discussed their frustrations that they began to find balance. Their story highlights a common issue: when communication about responsibilities is lacking, assumptions and misunderstandings fill the gaps, creating friction that erodes intimacy and trust.

But the mental load doesn't just affect our minds and relationships; it also manifests physically. Chronic stress from carrying the load can trigger headaches, migraines, and even sleep disturbances. Have you ever lain awake at night, running through tomorrow's to-do list, unable to quiet your mind? That's your mental load making itself known. Over time, this stress weakens your immune system, making you more susceptible to illnesses. I remember a friend who, after months of nonstop stress, found herself battling a persistent cold that refused to go away. "It was like my body was waving a white flag," she said. Prolonged stress can even lead to serious health issues like cardiovascular problems and mental health disorders, underscoring just how important it is to address this invisible burden.

One often-overlooked consequence of this stress is its ripple effect on how we parent or engage with loved ones. Exhaustion can lead to shorter tempers, less patience, and a diminished capacity to be fully present. A parent who feels emotionally depleted might find themselves snapping at their child over minor infractions or struggling to summon the energy for quality time. These moments of disconnection can build over time, creating emotional gaps that are hard to bridge. When our reserves are low, even acts of love and care can start to feel like obligations.

And let's not forget the role of societal expectations in all of this. Studies show that women, even in dual-income households, spend about 2.5 times more hours on unpaid household work than their male counterparts. These ingrained societal norms create a pervasive pressure to excel in both professional and domestic spheres, leaving many feeling they must perform flawlessly in every role. This imbalance isn't just anecdotal; it's statistically evident and reflects deeply rooted cultural narratives about gender and responsibility. We're surrounded by the myth of "having it all," perpetuated by social media's highlight reels. Every scroll through Instagram bombards us with picture-perfect families, spotless homes, and gourmet meals. It's no wonder so many of us feel like we're failing if we can't keep up. A friend once confided, "I look at those posts and think, 'Why can't I do that?' But the truth is, I'm barely holding it together." These pressures aren't just external;

they're deeply internalised, fueling perfectionism and guilt. The fear of judgment, of not being good enough, keeps us trapped in a cycle of overwork and self-doubt. And yet, these same platforms rarely show the reality behind the scenes—the meltdowns, the messes, and the moments of sheer overwhelm that make up real life.

Society's expectations also vary widely across cultures. In some, extended families share responsibilities, easing the mental load. In others, the burden falls squarely on one individual, often viewed as a badge of honour. I remember visiting a friend from a culture where asking for help was seen as weak. She admitted, "I'd rather struggle silently than let anyone think I can't handle it." This mindset only adds to the pressure, making it even harder to break free from the mental load. Contrast this with cultures that prioritise communal living and shared responsibilities, where tasks are naturally distributed among family members. These differences highlight how deeply societal norms shape our experiences of stress and support.

Then there's silent resentment—the hidden cost of an unbalanced mental load. For instance, I spoke with a couple who found themselves caught in this dynamic. The wife felt perpetually unseen as she managed everything from planning family vacations to ensuring bills were paid on time, while her husband assumed things were simply "handled." Their turning point came when she decided to voice her frustrations during a quiet evening. "I didn't realise how much you were doing," he admitted, shocked by the sheer volume of invisible work she listed. Together, they implemented a shared calendar and weekly check-ins, which not only redistributed tasks but also rekindled their mutual respect. This kind of open dialogue can be transformative, turning silent resentment into an opportunity for connection and growth. It's that unspoken frustration that simmers beneath the surface, building up until it spills over in unexpected ways. Maybe you snap at your partner for forgetting to take out the trash or feel a pang of bitterness when they don't notice your efforts. Silent resentment doesn't just harm relationships; it erodes trust and intimacy. A friend once shared how she felt invisible in her marriage because her efforts to keep their household running were never acknowledged. "It's like I'm a ghost," she said. Addressing this requires vulnerability and honest communication, which can be challenging but is ultimately essential for rebuilding connection.

So, where do we go from here? First, we acknowledge the impact of the mental load—on our minds, bodies, relationships, and overall well-being. Then, we take steps to lighten the burden. This isn't about fixing everything overnight; it's about small, sustainable changes. It's about setting boundaries, practicing self-care, and fostering open communication. It's about challenging societal norms and redefining what balance looks like for you. Above all, it's about giving yourself permission to share the load and let go of the guilt. Small acts, like delegating a task or voicing your needs, can begin to shift the dynamic in meaningful ways.

As we move forward, we'll explore practical strategies and real-life stories of people who've successfully navigated these challenges.

Because while the mental load is heavy, it's not unmovable. Together, we can find ways to carry it more evenly, creating space for joy, connection, and the freedom to simply breathe. Let's take that first step—together.

Chapter 3

Communication and Conflict Resolution

Have you ever tried to talk about how overwhelmed you feel, only to be met with a blank stare or a defensive response? Discussing the mental load isn't easy. It's the kind of conversation that can quickly spiral into frustration, misunderstandings, or worse, silence. But here's the truth: nothing will change unless you address it. You can't assume your partner knows what you're carrying unless you tell them. Imagine expecting your partner to notice the empty fridge or the unpaid bills piling up, only to feel disappointed when they don't. It's not that they don't care; they simply don't see the invisible work you're doing. For instance, a friend once told me about her frustration when her partner didn't realise their child's birthday party needed weeks of planning. When she finally brought it up, he admitted he assumed she "had it handled" because she didn't ask for help. This gap in understanding is why clear communication is so critical—it bridges the invisible divide and prevents resentment from taking root. The good news? Having this conversation doesn't have to feel like navigating a minefield. It starts with the right mindset and approach, one rooted in patience and empathy.

Imagine this: it's the end of a long day. You're mentally cataloging all the things you've done and the things still left undone. Your partner walks in, smiles, and says, "You seem stressed. What's going on?" It's an opening—an invitation to share—but how do you begin without it sounding like an attack? This is where starting with "I" statements comes in. For example: "I've been feeling overwhelmed trying to keep track of everything at home. I'd love to figure out a way we can manage things more evenly." Framing it this way focuses on your feelings and invites collaboration rather than assigning blame. It sets the tone for a discussion, not a confrontation.

Creating a safe space is essential. Choose a time when neither of you is rushed or distracted. For example, Sunday mornings over coffee might allow you time to talk without the stress of weekday obligations looming over you. Another example is car rides, discussing difficult topics side by side instead of face-to-face helped reduce tension. Whether it's during a relaxed dinner or a quiet evening walk, the key is choosing a setting where both of you feel comfortable and can engage openly without interruptions and that both of you feel heard and respected. Establishing simple ground rules, like taking turns speaking and avoiding interruptions, can make a world of difference. When you communicate with empathy, you're not just venting frustrations—you're fostering understanding. Think of it as setting the stage for a partnership rather than a performance review.

Empathetic language also plays a vital role. People often get defensive in these conversations because they feel criticized or unappreciated. When approached with blame, they may shut down or respond with frustration, making productive discussions difficult. This is why using empathetic language—framing concerns as shared challenges rather than personal failings—can transform a tense conversation into an opportunity for collaboration and understanding. Instead of saying, "You never help with the kids," try, "I've been struggling to keep up with the kids' schedules, and I'd really appreciate your help." This approach works because it reduces defensiveness and opens the door to collaboration. When language focuses on personal feelings and specific needs rather than blame, it creates an environment where both partners feel respected and are more likely to engage constructively. It shifts the focus from conflict to cooperation, making it easier to tackle the mental load as a team. Acknowledging your partner's efforts, no matter how small, can pave the way for more meaningful dialogue. "I noticed you folded the laundry last night—that was a huge help," goes a long way in setting a positive tone. Even small gestures of appreciation create a foundation for mutual respect and collaboration.

Once the conversation starts, listening becomes just as important as speaking. Active listening is about more than just hearing words; it's about understanding the emotions and intentions behind them.

If your partner is explaining how they've been feeling underappreciated, instead of planning your rebuttal, focus on their words, nod to show you're engaged, and paraphrase to confirm understanding. "It sounds like you're saying you feel overlooked when it comes to the work you do around the house—is that right?" This approach not only validates their feelings but also builds trust. Validation doesn't mean you have to agree, but it shows that you respect and acknowledge their perspective.

Barriers to effective listening often stem from distractions or preconceived notions. It's tempting to check your phone or let your mind wander, especially when the topic is challenging. But giving your full attention is crucial. Practicing mindful listening—staying present, acknowledging your emotions without letting them take over, and truly focusing on your partner's perspective—can transform the way you communicate. Imagine how different arguments might feel if both people felt genuinely heard.

Once you've opened the lines of communication, the next step is finding common ground. For instance, you may find you both have a shared goal to create more time for family dinners and you both agree that reducing weeknight chaos would help, so one partner takes over meal prep while the other manages the kids' after-school activities. Identifying this goal not only gives you both a sense of purpose but also makes the division of tasks feel meaningful and fair. Negotiating responsibilities isn't about winning or losing; it's about creating a partnership that works for both of you.

Start by identifying your shared goals. Maybe you both want a more peaceful home or more quality time together. Use these goals as a foundation to discuss how tasks can be divided. The key is to play to each other's strengths and preferences. Hate doing the dishes but don't mind folding laundry? Swap tasks to find balance. Balance doesn't have to mean equal; it means equitable and agreed upon by both parties.

Developing a task-sharing plan is a game-changer. Sit down together and list out all the responsibilities, big and small, that keep your household running. Categorise them by difficulty and time commitment, then allocate them in a way that feels fair. Remember, this isn't a one-and-done exercise. Regular check-ins to evaluate what's working and what isn't will help you adapt as life changes. Flexibility and open feedback ensure the plan remains sustainable. And don't be afraid to tweak the plan when life throws you curveballs—it's a sign of a healthy, adaptive partnership To help get you started, here are some suggested conversation starters:

- "I feel like I'm carrying a lot of the mental load at home, and I'd love to talk about how we can share it more evenly. What are your thoughts?"

- "Can we sit down and go through all the household responsibilities? I think it would help us both see what's getting done and where we might need to adjust."

- "I've noticed that I'm always the one planning the kids' activities and making sure everything runs smoothly. Could we find a way to share that responsibility more?"

- "What tasks do you feel you naturally take on at home, and which ones do you think I handle? Do you think this feels fair?"

- "I'm feeling really overwhelmed with everything on my plate, and I could use your support. Can we figure out a way to balance things better?"

- "How do you think we can divide household responsibilities in a way that plays to our strengths and schedules?"

- "What's one thing I do that you really appreciate? What's one thing I could do differently to make things feel more balanced?"

- "Can we set up a weekly or monthly check-in to talk about what's working and what isn't? I think it would help us stay on the same page."

- "What's something about managing a household that you didn't realize was so time-consuming until we talked about it?"

- "How do you think we can make household management more of a team effort instead of one person leading the charge?"

These conversation starters can help initiate productive discussions about the mental load, ensuring both partners feel heard and involved in creating a fairer system.

Even with the best intentions, conflict is inevitable. Disagreements about the mental load can feel deeply personal, but they don't have to become divisive. Understanding conflict dynamics is the first step. Recognising triggers—like feeling dismissed or overwhelmed—can help you approach disagreements with clarity. For example, if a fight escalates because one partner feels unappreciated, pause and address that feeling directly: "I'm sorry if my comment came across as dismissive. I value what you do, and I want us to work through this together." Conflict doesn't have to be destructive; it can be an opportunity for growth when approached constructively.

Transforming conflict into growth requires a mindset shift. For example, my husband and I constantly argued about household chores, with me feeling undervalued and him feeling micromanaged and nagged. Instead of letting resentment build, we tried to reframe our discussions to focus on shared goals rather than frustrations. By shifting our perspective from 'Who's doing more?' to 'How can we work together better?', we implemented a rotating task system that gave us both more flexibility and appreciation for each other's efforts. This shift in approach turned our conflicts into opportunities for mutual understanding and growth.

View arguments as opportunities to learn about each other's needs and perspectives. Techniques like taking a time-out to cool down or approaching the issue with a "win-win" mentality can de-escalate tension. Instead of aiming to be right, aim to find a solution that benefits you both.

Finally, make regular check-ins a priority. Aim to have these conversations weekly or biweekly, depending on your household's needs. A short, structured chat over coffee on a Sunday morning or during a relaxed evening walk can be enough to identify issues before they escalate. The key is consistency—regular check-ins create a habit of open communication and ensure both partners feel heard and supported. Use simple prompts like, "What's been working well for us this week?" or "Is there anything you'd like more help with?" These questions open the door for honest dialogue and help uncover small frustrations before they grow into bigger issues. Keeping it casual but purposeful ensures these check-ins feel supportive rather than stressful.

Talking about the mental load isn't a one-time conversation—it's an ongoing dialogue. With empathy, active listening, and a willingness to adapt, you can turn these discussions into a cornerstone of a healthier, more balanced partnership. By making space for these conversations, you're not just addressing the mental load—you're building a relationship that thrives on understanding, respect, and shared purpose.

Chapter 4
Strategies for Equitable Task Distribution

Let's be honest: dividing household tasks equitably can feel like trying to assemble flat-pack furniture without instructions. You're bound to encounter frustration, and someone inevitably ends up holding the metaphorical Allen wrench while wondering where it all went wrong. But when you find a system that works, the result is a more harmonious home and a lot less resentment. A successful system is one that feels intuitive and adaptable, balancing the unique strengths and schedules of everyone involved. It prioritizes clear communication, regular check-ins, and flexibility to handle the unexpected. At its core, such a system fosters mutual respect and accountability, ensuring that both partners feel their contributions are valued and meaningful. Achieving this harmony isn't just about logistics—it's about creating a partnership built on trust, understanding, and a shared vision for how life can run more smoothly. And the truth is, when both partners feel valued and supported, the entire household thrives.

Shared responsibility models are a great place to start. Think of these as frameworks you can tailor to your unique relationship dynamics. Some couples swear by rotational schedules—taking turns with tasks like cooking or laundry to keep things fair. Others prefer time-based sharing, such as alternating who handles morning versus evening responsibilities. Then there's strengths-based distribution, where each partner takes on tasks they're naturally better at or enjoy more. For example, if one of you is a whiz at budgeting but loathes grocery shopping, you can divide tasks accordingly. The key is flexibility. No single model fits every household, but by experimenting, you'll discover what works best for you—and you'll both feel less overwhelmed.

Take Sarah and Tom, for instance. Both work full-time and found themselves constantly bickering over who was doing more around the house. They started by writing down every household task they could think of, from walking the dog to paying bills. Then, over coffee on a Saturday morning, they began experimenting with different ways to divide the workload. At first, they tried alternating days for cooking and cleaning but found it wasn't sustainable with their work schedules. Eventually, they shifted to a strengths-based approach: Sarah's flair for organization made her the go-to person for planning meals and shopping lists, while Tom took on tasks requiring efficiency, like doing the dishes and managing the family budget. They didn't just split tasks—they played to their strengths, making the workload feel fair and manageable. The process wasn't perfect, but each trial brought them closer to a system that felt fair. Now, they regularly revisit their arrangement to ensure it still works as life changes, keeping their household running smoothly and their relationship stronger. Over time, they found that this system not only reduced their arguments but also gave them more time to enjoy each other's company—a win-win. They even noticed a surprising side effect: their kids started mirroring this teamwork, taking on small chores without being asked.

A more structured approach is the Household CEO concept, which takes task ownership to another level. Here, instead of sharing every task, you assign "domains" to each partner. Think of it as running a company: one partner might oversee "operations" (cooking, cleaning), while the other handles "finances" (budgeting, bills). By owning specific areas, each person gains clarity about their responsibilities, reducing micromanagement and overlap. This model works especially well for couples who feel overwhelmed by constant negotiations about who's doing what, as it eliminates the guesswork and empowers each person to lead their respective domains with confidence.

I remember speaking with a friend who implemented this system with her partner. She became the CEO of household maintenance, handling everything from hiring plumbers to fixing leaky faucets. Meanwhile, her partner took charge of scheduling—coordinating school activities, medical appointments, and social events. She admitted that at first, it felt weird to relinquish control, but once she saw how much smoother things ran, she never looked back. Task ownership fosters accountability and pride, but it also requires trust and open communication to address any gaps or overlaps.

Couples who embrace this approach often report feeling more empowered and less burdened by the mental load. It also builds a sense of accomplishment, as each partner can see the tangible impact of their contributions.

Of course, in today's tech-savvy world, practical tools can make all the difference. For example, we use a shared app to coordinate our grocery shopping. Each time one of us notices an item running low, we add it to the list, and whoever has time would pick up the items during their next store visit has access to the list so no one item is forgotten. This simple tool eliminated our frequent miscommunications about what was needed and ensured that tasks were evenly distributed without constant reminders. By integrating technology into our routine, we not only streamlined our household management but also reduced stress and arguments about forgotten errands.

Apps like Trello or Asana aren't just for office use; they can streamline household management too. Shared calendars, like Google Calendar, help ensure you're both on the same page about appointments and deadlines. Home automation systems can even take over mundane tasks, like reminding you to reorder household essentials or turning off the lights at night. The trick is finding tools that integrate seamlessly into your routine. Start small: set up a shared grocery list or use an app to track weekly chores. The less effort it takes to maintain the system, the more likely you are to stick with it. And remember, technology is a tool, not a solution. It's there to support your efforts, not replace the need for communication and collaboration. One couple I know swears by a shared app that sends reminders for birthdays, anniversaries, and even recurring bills, saving them countless arguments over forgotten dates.

Then there's the Fair Play system, which takes task division to an entirely new level. Popularized by Eve Rodsky, this method involves creating a "deck" of all household tasks and dividing them equitably based on effort, not just time. The process begins with an inventory of everything that needs to be done—yes, everything. From scheduling doctor's appointments to remembering Grandma's birthday, no task is too small. Once you've laid it all out, you discuss and assign responsibilities, ensuring that both partners feel the division is fair. Regular check-ins to reevaluate and adjust keep the system running smoothly. The beauty of Fair Play is its ability to make the invisible visible, giving both partners a clearer understanding of the workload. One couple who adopted this method told me that it was like "finally turning on a light in a room we'd been fumbling around in for years." They noticed an immediate decrease in tension and a stronger sense of teamwork.

Life, of course, is anything but static. The arrival of a new baby, a career change, or even a long-term visitor can throw even the best-laid plans into chaos. But sometimes, it's the smaller disruptions—like a car breaking down or an unexpected work deadline—that can make an already precarious balance feel overwhelming. One couple shared how an unplanned power outage during a busy week forced them to rearrange their evening routines, prompting a discussion about flexibility and how they could better support each other when the unexpected happens. These moments, while challenging, can also be opportunities to strengthen your system and learn how to adapt on the fly. That's why flexibility is key. Revisiting your task-sharing system during major life transitions can prevent tension and ensure the load remains balanced. I know a couple who temporarily swapped roles after the husband was laid off. While job hunting, he took over household management, giving his wife space to focus on her demanding job. Once he was back to work, they adjusted again, proving that adaptability is the secret to long-term success. Change is inevitable, but a flexible system ensures you're both prepared to meet it. Another family I spoke to restructured their system entirely after deciding to homeschool their children, demonstrating how even the most dramatic shifts can be navigated with thoughtful planning.

Finally, don't underestimate the power of long-term planning. Setting goals together, like saving for a home renovation or planning an annual family vacation, helps align your priorities and gives context to your shared responsibilities. It's not just about getting through the daily grind; it's about building a life that reflects your values and aspirations. Think of your task-sharing system as a living, breathing agreement—one that evolves as your needs and circumstances change. Regularly revisiting these goals can help keep both partners motivated and invested in the partnership. Set aside an evening every quarter to dream big, assess your progress, and make adjustments, turning what could feel like a chore into a shared celebration of your growth.

Equitable task distribution isn't about achieving perfect balance every day. It's about creating a partnership where both people feel valued, supported, and empowered to contribute. Think back to Sarah and Tom, who used their strengths to find a system that worked for them. Their willingness to adapt and play to each other's skills reinforced their sense of mutual respect and fairness. By linking shared goals with tailored solutions, they not only divided the workload but also strengthened their connection—a testament to how equitable systems can transform a household. Whether you're experimenting with shared responsibility models, embracing the Household CEO concept, or leveraging the latest tech, the goal is the same: to lighten the load and strengthen your connection. By working together, you're not just dividing tasks—you're building a foundation for a more harmonious and fulfilling life. And when the balance tips occasionally, as it inevitably will, you'll have the tools and trust to tip it back again. It's not just about managing your home—it's about thriving together as a team.

Chapter 5

Emotional and Cognitive Load Management

Have you ever felt like your brain is running a marathon while your body is just trying to make it to the end of the day? The physical toll of this constant stress can manifest in headaches, muscle tension, and chronic fatigue, while the mental strain can lead to anxiety, burnout, and even depression. Managing the emotional and cognitive load in our daily lives is no small feat. It's the unseen effort of keeping everything running—from being the family's emotional support system to juggling a never-ending mental to-do list. These responsibilities, while often invisible, can manifest in daily life as constant fatigue, difficulty concentrating, and a creeping sense of overwhelm. For many, it looks like staying up late to finish tasks no one else notices or feeling irritable during interactions because your mental reserves are drained. Relationships often bear the brunt, with unspoken resentments building as one partner feels unseen or unsupported. This unseen effort impacts not only individual mental health but also the dynamics within families.

Over time, unaddressed stress can contribute to serious mental health struggles, including panic attacks, sleep disorders, and emotional detachment. The effects ripple outward, straining relationships and making even small conflicts feel overwhelming, which is why it's crucial to address and share the load before reaching a breaking point. But here's the good news: with intentional strategies, it's possible to lighten this burden and create a more balanced, fulfilling life. Through small but meaningful changes, you can take control of the emotional and cognitive demands that so often weigh you down.

Emotional Check-Ins: Building Empathy and Connection

Regular emotional check-ins are like tuning the engine of a car—they keep your relationship running smoothly. These aren't grand therapy sessions; they're simple, intentional conversations designed to foster empathy and connection. Setting aside time weekly or bi-weekly for these check-ins can create a safe space where both partners feel comfortable sharing their thoughts and feelings without fear of judgment or interruption.

Start with open-ended questions: "How have you been feeling about our routines lately?" or "What's been weighing on your mind this week?" For example, one couple discovered that asking these questions during their evening walks led to insights about how they could better support each other's work schedules. The husband shared that he felt overwhelmed managing morning routines, while the wife realized she could take on more of the prep to ease his stress. By identifying these pain points, they made small adjustments that significantly improved their daily flow and emotional connection. The goal is to encourage vulnerability without judgment. For example, finding success in your check-ins by sharing "three good things and one challenge" from your week, opening the door to meaningful discussions. You can also use a structured approach, taking turns to share highlights and low points of your day, ensuring both partners have equal opportunities to speak. These conversations help identify stressors, unmet emotional needs, and areas where support is most needed. Over time, they build trust and deepen understanding, reinforcing the bond between partners. Emotional check-ins are not only tools for connection but also powerful reminders that your relationship is a partnership built on mutual care and empathy.

Boundary Setting: Protecting Your Emotional Bandwidth

Boundaries are the unsung heroes of emotional well-being. They're often overlooked because many people struggle to recognize where they're needed or fear that setting limits will disappoint others. Additionally, societal expectations, like the pressure to be constantly available or to prioritize others' needs over your own, can make implementing boundaries feel selfish or uncomfortable. However, these misconceptions only underscore the importance of boundaries in maintaining emotional health and ensuring sustainable relationships. They define where your responsibilities end and someone else's begin, giving you the space to recharge and maintain your emotional bandwidth. Think of them as the guardrails that keep your mental health from veering off course.

Without boundaries, the lines between your needs and others' demands can blur, leading to burnout and resentment.

Start by identifying areas where you feel stretched too thin. Perhaps you've been fielding work emails late into the evening or taking on more than your fair share of household tasks. Once you've pinpointed these areas, communicate your boundaries clearly: "I need to stop checking emails after 7 p.m. so I can unwind in the evenings." Similarly, setting boundaries with extended family or friends—like limiting unplanned visits—can help protect your emotional bandwidth. Remember, boundaries aren't about shutting people out; they're about protecting your energy and prioritizing what matters most.

Respecting your partner's boundaries is just as crucial. One couple I spoke with found harmony by agreeing to dedicate Sundays to family time, free from work interruptions. They also made a pact to avoid discussing stressful topics after 9 p.m., recognizing the importance of preserving their evening as a time to unwind. When boundaries are crossed—as they inevitably will be—approach the situation calmly. Reaffirm your needs and collaboratively find ways to honor them moving forward. Boundaries aren't rigid walls; they're flexible agreements that adapt as your circumstances change. By continuously revisiting and respecting each other's boundaries, you can create a household environment that feels supportive and balanced.

Mindfulness Practices: Staying Present and Balanced

Mindfulness is more than a trendy buzzword; it's a powerful tool for managing stress and staying grounded amid life's chaos. At its core, mindfulness is about living in the present moment with full awareness of your thoughts and emotions. It helps you break free from the constant cycle of worry and multitasking, giving you the clarity to focus on what truly matters. While mindfulness won't erase stress, it changes your relationship with it, helping you navigate life's challenges with greater ease.

Start small. Incorporate mindfulness into daily activities like eating or walking. For instance, savor the taste of your morning coffee or pay attention to the rhythm of your breath during a stroll. Techniques like breathing exercises, meditation, and body scanning can also help reduce stress. A friend of mine who has 6 kids shared how a five-minute breathing practice each morning transformed her ability to stay calm during hectic school drop-offs. She made it part of her routine by setting an alarm ten minutes earlier than usual and finding a quiet spot in the kitchen before the morning chaos began. Focusing on slow, deep breaths, she found that this brief moment of mindfulness helped reset her mindset for the day. Over time, it became a cherished ritual that not only reduced stress but also set a positive tone for managing the rest of the morning's demands. Another found solace in mindful journaling, writing down three things they were grateful for each evening, which helped them end the day on a positive note.

Mindfulness isn't about eliminating stress but about changing your relationship with it. By practicing regularly, you'll find it easier to manage emotional ups and downs, improve focus, and approach challenges with a clearer mind. Families can benefit too—introducing mindfulness practices like a five-minute family meditation before dinner can create moments of calm and connection in an otherwise busy household.

Cognitive Offloading: Tools to Lighten the Mental Load

The mental load can feel like a weight that never lifts, constantly demanding attention and mental energy. Cognitive offloading provides a practical way to reduce this burden by shifting mental tasks to external systems, freeing up space in your mind for creativity, problem-solving, and relaxation. At its essence, cognitive offloading involves transferring mental tasks to external systems so your brain has room to breathe. Imagine not having to remember every detail because you've got reliable tools to keep track of them for you. Cognitive offloading isn't about shirking responsibilities; it's about making space for creativity, focus, and relaxation.

Start with simple techniques like to-do lists and schedules. Digital tools like Todoist or Evernote can be game-changers, helping you organize tasks and set reminders. For example, my family use a shared digital calendar to keep track of appointments, meal plans, and even chore rotations. We found that having everything in one place reduced miscommunications and eased the mental burden. Some families swear by having a physical command center in their kitchen, complete with a whiteboard for weekly goals, a calendar, and space for sticky notes about urgent tasks.

Technology is a helpful ally, but it's not the only solution. While apps and automation can streamline tasks, relying too heavily on technology can sometimes overcomplicate simple routines or create new frustrations. For example, if a shared task app sends too many notifications, it might feel like more of a burden than a relief. The key is to find a balance—using technology as a tool to support your efforts rather than replacing essential communication and collaboration. The key is finding tools that integrate seamlessly into your routine, reducing stress without creating more work. Experiment with different methods to see what fits your lifestyle best. And don't forget to involve your partner and family members in the process; when everyone shares responsibility for maintaining these systems, the load becomes lighter for all.

Support Networks: Building Your Emotional Safety Net

No one can do it all alone, and that's where "the village" comes in. I never hesitate to ask for help from my family and friends when scheduling conflicts arise. This kind of support system has existed for centuries—families and communities have always relied on each other to share responsibilities, lighten burdens, and provide emotional reinforcement. When you have a network to lean on, you not only feel supported, but you gain a sense of security, knowing that you won't be left to juggle everything alone. There is a reciprocal nature to this—it's not just about asking for help, but also about offering support when others need it. And when you know help is there when you need it, the weight of the mental load feels lighter, and the fear of failure diminishes. For example, I spoke with a working mother who leaned on her close-knit group of friends during a particularly stressful period. They organized a meal train, helped with school pickups, and checked in regularly to offer emotional support. This collective effort not only eased her burden but also deepened her relationships with those around her. Stories like hers highlight how invaluable a strong support network can be for navigating life's challenges. A strong network of friends, family, and professionals can be a lifeline for managing emotional labor and preventing burnout. These are the people who listen without judgment, offer perspective, and step in when you need extra help. Building and maintaining these relationships is essential for long-term emotional health.

Start by identifying key supporters in your life. Maybe it's a friend who always knows the right thing to say or a family member who's great at pitching in during busy times. Professional support, like a therapist or life coach, can also provide invaluable tools for navigating challenges. One parent I know leaned heavily on a local parenting group during a particularly tough year, finding both practical advice and emotional camaraderie. Another relied on a neighbor's kindness for after-school pickups, proving that support often comes from unexpected places.

Engaging with your support network doesn't have to be formal. Regular check-ins, coffee dates, or even a quick text exchange can help you feel connected and less isolated. If you're someone who hesitates to ask for help, start small—like requesting a favor or sharing a challenge with someone you trust. Balance is key; while seeking support is vital, maintaining a sense of independence ensures you stay in control of your own journey. Remember, support networks aren't just about receiving help; they're about creating reciprocal relationships where everyone benefits.

Managing the emotional and cognitive load isn't about erasing stress—it's about creating systems and practices that make it manageable. By prioritizing emotional check-ins, setting boundaries, embracing mindfulness, offloading mental tasks, and leaning on your support network, you can transform the way you navigate life's demands. These strategies don't just lighten the load; they create space for joy, connection, and the freedom to focus on what truly matters. Over time, you'll find that these intentional practices not only make life easier but also enrich your relationships and overall well-being.

Chapter 6

Overcoming Obstacles and Objections

Introducing changes in managing the mental load can sometimes meet resistance, particularly if one partner doesn't fully grasp the concept or fears how it might impact them. Understanding why your partner might be skeptical is the first step in overcoming this obstacle. Resistance often stems from concerns—whether it's anxiety over increased responsibilities, hesitation about disrupting routines, or a simple misunderstanding of what the mental load entails. These fears are common because they tap into deeply ingrained habits and roles that feel comfortable, even if they're unbalanced. For instance, a partner might worry that shared responsibilities mean less personal downtime or increased pressure to meet new expectations. This apprehension can create a defensive reaction, making the idea of change feel like a threat rather than an opportunity for growth. For instance, a partner might view the discussion as criticism rather than an opportunity for growth, leading to defensiveness.

To bridge this gap, communication is key. Share personal experiences and feelings to help your partner understand why this conversation is important. Managing the children's schedules can often feel overwhelming and invisible. The constant coordination of school events, extracurricular activities, and medical appointments can become an exhausting mental burden when not acknowledged or shared. Expressing these feelings in a way that fosters understanding—such as discussing the impact of this responsibility on daily stress levels—can open the door for a more balanced distribution of tasks. By framing your feelings rather than assigning blame, you can create a safe space for dialogue. Presenting factual information, such as studies showing the benefits of shared responsibilities on relationship satisfaction, can also help clarify the value of change.

Empathy is a powerful tool in these discussions. Walking through each other's daily routines can highlight invisible tasks one partner might not notice. Acknowledge and validate their concerns, showing that you understand their hesitations. For instance, you might say, "I know this feels like a big shift, but I think we can find a way that works for both of us." Involving your partner in crafting solutions—like co-creating a task-sharing plan or setting mutual goals—can transform skepticism into collaboration. You might find success by sitting down together to map out your daily responsibilities, opening your eyes to the uneven distribution of invisible labor and inspiring a shared commitment to change.

One of the most common objections to managing the mental load is time. I remember when I worked in the corporate world, leaving the office at 4:30 p.m. to pick up my kids. The shame I felt as I packed up my things, as if I didn't care about my career, was overwhelming. But the reality was that someone had to pick them up, and my husband, working long hours as a consultant, wasn't going to be the one to do it. The weight of that unspoken expectation sat heavily on me, and eventually, it became one of the reasons I changed careers to teaching—it offered the flexibility I needed to balance work and family life. Societal expectations often reinforce these constraints, with traditional gender roles dictating that women should handle household responsibilities even when working full-time. Meanwhile, men may feel pressure to prioritize work obligations, making it difficult to engage in domestic tasks. These ingrained dynamics can make it challenging to carve out time for redistributing responsibilities, reinforcing patterns that leave one partner overwhelmed. In a world where schedules are already packed, finding room to implement new strategies can feel impossible. The solution lies in analyzing how time is currently spent and identifying opportunities for improvement. Begin with a simple time-tracking exercise. For one week, note how you and your partner allocate your time. Are there pockets of inefficiency or activities that could be streamlined? I know my family acknowledged that mornings were consistently chaotic because tasks like making lunches and finding keys weren't assigned, prompting us to create a checklist for smoother starts and go organise these tasks the day before.

Once you've analyzed your time usage, prioritize tasks using tools like the Eisenhower Box, which categorizes tasks as urgent, important, or non-essential. Weekly planning sessions can also help you align your schedules and create a "must-do" list that ensures essential tasks are completed first. My husband and I were struggling to stay on top of our household chores so we began holding 15-minute planning sessions every Sunday evening. During these sessions, we outline our top priorities for the week and divided tasks based on availability. This routine not only reduced missed deadlines but also gave us a clearer sense of shared responsibility, transforming our chaotic weeks into a smoother flow.

Streamlining routines is another effective approach. Batch process similar tasks, such as meal prep or errands, to save time. Delegate non-essential tasks to other family members or even outsource them if feasible. Technology can be a game-changer here—calendar apps with shared access or automation tools that handle recurring tasks can free up mental bandwidth. The introduction of online grocery shopping with recurring orders has completely transformed how we manage our household, saving valuable time each week and reducing the stress of last-minute grocery runs. Meal planning apps can also help to coordinate dinners, drastically reducing last-minute decision fatigue.

No two relationships are identical, and unique circumstances often require tailored strategies for managing the mental load. Whether you're navigating a long-distance relationship, balancing shift work, or accommodating cultural differences, finding a customized approach is key.

Begin by recognizing the unique challenges you face. For example, if one partner works nights while the other has a traditional 9-to-5 job, dividing tasks equally might not be feasible. Instead, consider flexible task-sharing arrangements that account for availability and energy levels. Personalized communication techniques, like regular video calls for long-distance couples, can help maintain connection and alignment.

Incorporating diverse needs into your solutions is equally important. For centuries, cultures have adapted and evolved their approaches to household roles, emphasizing shared efforts within families and communities. A couple from different cultural backgrounds might approach household responsibilities differently, making open dialogue essential to reconcile expectations. For example, one couple found success by creating a shared document listing all household tasks, assigning them based on preferences and availability. This allowed them to respect their individual traditions while creating a fair and efficient system.

Taking an iterative approach—testing strategies, gathering feedback, and adjusting—ensures that solutions remain effective over time. Celebrating small victories, such as successfully implementing a new chore rotation or reducing the frequency of last-minute conflicts, reinforces motivation. Acknowledging progress openly, such as saying, "We're doing so much better at this than we were a month ago," fosters confidence and strengthens the partnership. Knowing that support is reciprocated helps both partners feel more secure, reinforcing the idea that they are working together rather than alone.

Change is intimidating, even when it promises improvement. Fear of failure, fear of disrupting routines, or simply stepping into the unknown can make embracing new strategies challenging. To address these fears, start small. Implement one manageable change at a time, such as using a shared calendar or setting aside a weekly check-in.

Early successes build confidence. For instance, one couple began by sharing meal planning duties, finding that even this small adjustment reduced stress and fostered teamwork. Creating a supportive environment is also crucial. External support systems, such as friends and family, can play a significant role in reducing resistance to change. When household responsibilities are normalized as shared efforts (remember the village?), rather than falling on one person, it becomes easier for partners to embrace new strategies. Seeking advice from trusted friends who have successfully navigated similar changes or involving extended family in certain responsibilities can provide reinforcement and encouragement. A well-supported shift feels less daunting, and knowing there is a network to lean on fosters confidence in sustaining new habits. Encourage open dialogue about fears, and celebrate adaptability and resilience. Remind each other that change is a process, not a destination. Our family introduced a Sunday evening check-in to reflect on our progress and plan the week ahead, creating a new tradition that reinforced our shared goals.

Mindset shifts can make all the difference. View challenges as opportunities for growth rather than setbacks. For example, if you initially struggle with task-sharing because it disrupts your established routines, try not to focus on the disruption, but choose to see it as a chance to redefine your partnership. By approaching challenges with curiosity, you can began experimenting with different strategies, like rotating responsibilities every month. This shift in perspective helps you see the process as a collaborative effort, fostering a sense of teamwork and mutual respect rather than frustration. Reframe difficulties as learning experiences, emphasizing the long-term benefits of shared responsibility. Many people initially struggle with task-sharing, often perceiving it as an added burden rather than an opportunity for partnership. However, shifting the mindset—from seeing the effort as a chore to recognizing it as an investment in a healthier, more balanced relationship—can make all the difference. Rather than striving for perfection, focusing on incremental improvements fosters a sense of progress. The key is to embrace collaboration as an evolving process, where adjustments are made along the way to create a fairer and more sustainable system.

Consistency is the foundation of lasting change. Establishing new habits and routines takes effort, but the payoff is well worth it. Start by setting clear, attainable goals. Book in that weekly planning session with your spouse every Sunday evening now! Use habit-tracking tools or apps to monitor progress and maintain accountability.

Accountability can take many forms. Partner check-ins or even involving accountability groups can help reinforce new behaviors. Positive reinforcement—like celebrating small wins—keeps motivation high. For instance, one couple celebrated their progress by creating a "wall of wins" in their kitchen, where they jotted down every accomplishment, big or small, on sticky notes. This visible reminder not only motivated them but also fostered a sense of pride in their shared efforts, making the process of change more rewarding and fun. Reward yourselves with a monthly date night for sticking to your new task-sharing plan. Create a reward chart for your children, teaching them the value of shared effort and teamwork.

Setbacks are inevitable, but they don't have to derail progress. If you initially struggle to maintain your new task-sharing system when work deadlines and family obligations increased, instead of reverting to old habits, pause to reassess your approach. Try to temporarily shift responsibilities and add a mid-week check-in to ensure neither partner feels overwhelmed. By acknowledging the challenge and adjusting your strategy, you prevent frustration from building and keep your momentum going. Treat them as opportunities to adjust your strategies and realign your goals. One couple, faced with a particularly chaotic month, revisited their chore assignments and made temporary adjustments to better accommodate their schedules. Remember, the journey to a balanced mental load isn't linear, but with consistency and adaptability, it's achievable. By committing to these changes, you're not only improving your daily life but also laying the groundwork for a stronger, more equitable partnership.

Chapter 7

Exercises and Tools for Change

Relationship Equity Exercises: Building Fairness Together

Creating fairness in a relationship doesn't happen by chance—it requires intentional effort and shared commitment. Relationship equity exercises are a powerful way to bring hidden imbalances to light and foster a sense of teamwork. These exercises focus on task sharing and help both partners recognize areas where one person may be shouldering more than their fair share.

Structured activities like "A Day in My Shoes" can provide a valuable perspective shift. This role-reversal exercise allows partners to swap responsibilities for a day, experiencing firsthand what the other manages. For instance, one couple used this exercise to swap their weekday routines. The husband, who had never managed school drop-offs or after-school activities, gained a newfound respect for the logistical challenges involved. Meanwhile, the wife realized how mentally exhausting it was to juggle a high-stress job while keeping track of home maintenance schedules.

These realizations not only increased empathy but also inspired them to divide tasks more thoughtfully. In this role-reversal exercise, partners swap responsibilities for a day, experiencing what the other manages. One couple found this particularly impactful when the husband realized how much effort went into managing the children's schedules, a task he had previously underestimated. Another engaging activity, "Balance the Scales," involves listing household tasks and categorizing them by time and effort. This game-like approach highlights imbalances and prompts meaningful conversations about redistribution.

For these exercises to succeed, joint participation is essential. Set aside regular times to engage in these activities, creating a comfortable environment where both partners feel open to learning and growing. Reflecting on the outcomes together deepens the impact. Discussing insights and adjusting strategies based on these realizations can lead to lasting change and a stronger partnership. Additionally, these exercises often spark moments of mutual appreciation, as partners begin to see each other's contributions in a new light, fostering gratitude and respect.

Task Audit: Identifying Invisible Work

The mental load often includes countless invisible tasks that go unnoticed but are essential for a household's functioning. Conducting a task audit can help uncover these hidden responsibilities and provide clarity on how they're distributed. It's a vital first step toward addressing imbalances and ensuring tasks are shared more equitably.

Start by listing all daily, weekly, and monthly tasks. To help get you started have a look at the tasks listed on page 89. Categorize them by type—like cleaning, scheduling, or emotional labor—and assess the time and effort required for each. Highlight activities that often go unrecognized, such as remembering family birthdays or keeping track of medical appointments. This process not only brings transparency but also validates the effort involved in managing these responsibilities.

Digital tools like task tracking templates or spreadsheet apps can simplify the process. Apps like Trello, Todoist, and Microsoft To Do help with organizing tasks and setting reminders, while Google Sheets or Notion can serve as collaborative spaces for managing household responsibilities. These tools provide visual clarity and accountability, making it easier to track progress and adjust as needed. For example, one family used a shared Google Sheet to list and allocate chores, making it easier to visualize who was doing what. Once the audit is complete, use the results to inform new strategies. Redistribute tasks that feel disproportionately assigned, and create action plans to address any imbalances. Regularly revisiting the audit ensures that the system evolves with your needs. Aim to conduct a task audit at least once every three to six months, or whenever there's a significant life change, like starting a new job or welcoming a new family member. My family noticed a growing imbalance after our youngest child started school, prompting us to reassess and redistribute tasks like transportation and homework help. Regular reviews help ensure fairness and adaptability as circumstances shift. Moreover, conducting periodic audits can highlight areas of improvement, allowing you to celebrate progress and fine-tune your strategies.

Communication Drills: Practicing Effective Dialogue

Good communication is the backbone of any strong relationship, but it takes practice to master. Communication drills are practical exercises designed to enhance dialogue and deepen understanding between partners. They build confidence in expressing needs and foster active listening skills, creating a foundation for better collaboration.

Try exercises like the "Five-Minute Exchange," where each partner speaks uninterrupted for five minutes about their feelings while the other listens attentively. "I Feel" statements ("I feel stressed when I'm the only one planning meals") are another effective tool for expressing emotions without assigning blame. The "Mirror and Reflect" drill encourages paraphrasing to ensure understanding: "What I hear you saying is that you feel overwhelmed managing the kids' schedules. Is that right?"

Setting up practice sessions in a distraction-free environment is key. This means finding a quiet, uninterrupted space where both partners can focus without distractions like phones, television, or children needing attention. You might find that having your discussions during an evening walk helps you engage more openly, while others might prefer setting aside time after dinner when the house is calmer. Choosing the right environment ensures that both partners can be fully present and engaged in the conversation.

Establish clear objectives for each session, like improving listening skills or addressing a specific issue. Reflect on progress by journaling after each drill or seeking feedback from your partner. Over time, these exercises can transform how you communicate, turning difficult conversations into opportunities for growth. My husband and I found that integrating these drills into our weekly routine not only improved our communication but also strengthened our emotional connection, as we felt more understood and valued by one another.

Emotional Load Journal: Tracking Progress

The emotional load is often hard to quantify, but maintaining an emotional load journal can help track your progress in managing it. This journal serves as a space to reflect on emotional states, identify triggers, and monitor improvements over time.

Start by choosing a format that suits you—whether it's a digital app or a traditional notebook. Establish a regular journaling routine, perhaps at the end of each day or week. Use prompts like "What emotions did I experience today?" or "What tasks felt most overwhelming?" to guide your entries. For example, one parent noted that evenings were their most stressful time, prompting them to adjust their family's dinner and bedtime routines to reduce strain.

Reflecting on journal insights can facilitate growth. Reviewing your journal entries weekly or biweekly can help you track patterns, identify recurring stressors, and adjust your approach before small issues become overwhelming. Regular check-ins with yourself—or even with your partner—ensure that progress remains steady and adjustments are made as needed. Look for patterns, such as recurring stressors or moments when you felt supported. Use these reflections to adjust strategies and advocate for changes that improve your emotional well-being. For example, you might discover through your journal entries that the lack of a consistent morning routine is a major stressor. By establishing a simple plan, including preparing clothes and lunches the night before, you can significantly reduced your morning anxiety. Sharing these findings with your partner will lead to a collaborative effort to refine your household routines, further easing the emotional load. Over time, this practice not only lightens the emotional load but also enhances your ability to navigate challenges with resilience. Some journalers have also found it helpful to share key insights with their partners, using the journal as a tool to foster collaboration and mutual understanding.

Vision Board: Creating a Shared Future

A vision board is a creative and inspiring tool for visualizing a shared future. By collaboratively setting goals and aspirations, partners can align their efforts and stay motivated. This process encourages creative expression and strengthens the bond between partners.

Begin by collecting images, quotes, and symbols that represent your shared goals, whether it's planning a dream vacation, saving for a home, or achieving better work-life balance. Arrange and assemble the board together, using it as an opportunity to discuss your aspirations. Include relationship-specific goals, like improving communication or redistributing household tasks.

Display the vision board prominently as a daily reminder of your shared journey. Choose a location where both partners will see it frequently, such as the kitchen, bedroom, or a shared workspace. Make it interactive by leaving space for new ideas or tracking milestones along the way. Consider adding sticky notes for short-term goals, a section for accomplishments, or even a rotating focus area where you highlight a priority for the month. For couples who prefer a digital approach, consider using apps or creating a shared folder with images and updates to keep your vision board accessible on all devices. These visible reminders can serve as daily inspiration, reinforcing your commitment to achieving shared goals and celebrating progress along the way. Choose a location where both partners will see it frequently, such as the kitchen, bedroom, or a shared workspace. For couples who prefer a digital approach, consider using apps or creating a shared folder with images and updates to keep your vision board accessible on all devices. These visible reminders can serve as daily inspiration, reinforcing your commitment to achieving shared goals and celebrating progress along the way. Regularly review and update it as your goals evolve, celebrating milestones along the way. One couple added a section for completed goals, creating a tangible record of their progress and a source of encouragement for future endeavors. By keeping your vision board alive and dynamic, it becomes a powerful motivator for continuous growth and connection. Some couples have taken this a step further by creating mini vision boards for specific areas of their lives, such as career, parenting, or health, ensuring that their aspirations remain well-rounded and inclusive.

Chapter 8

Real Couples, Real Solutions: Stories of Change

Like many, my journey with the mental load has been filled with ups and downs. Early in my career, I struggled to balance the demands of work and home life. I vividly remember a moment of clarity when, after a particularly stressful week, I realized I was carrying far too much on my own. It wasn't just about tasks; it was about the emotional toll of being the default manager of everything. I would wake of a morning already mentally and physically exhausted, despite the fact I had had a restful 8 hours sleep. My husband thought that being the "bread winner" and having a stressful job let him off doing his fair share of tasks around the house because financially he was contributing. He'd do the stereotypical jobs around the house that men would do, like mow the lawn and put the bins out, but if he did anything beyond that it was as if he was doing me a favor. I defaulted to just doing it all as it was easier to do it then ask for help and have to explain to him that the middle child will have cheese sticks in her lunch but not sliced cheese in her sandwich, and that the eldest child needs to wear her sports uniform today but the youngest two need to wear their formal uniform and the middle child had violin practise today....the list goes on.

The turning point came when I began to set boundaries. I started small: designating specific hours for work and family and prioritizing self-care without guilt. Another game-changer was listing all the jobs that I do and communicating that to my partner. Simple weekly check-ins transformed how we managed our shared responsibilities, fostering a sense of teamwork rather than resentment. These conversations often revealed overlooked challenges, like how we both felt overwhelmed by different parts of our routines, and together, we found creative solutions.

Mindfulness practices became my anchor. A few minutes of meditation (over coffee) each morning helped me navigate the chaos with greater clarity by fostering a sense of calm and focus. This practice allowed me to approach my to-do list with a clearer head, prioritizing tasks more effectively and reducing the anxiety of feeling overwhelmed. It also improved my interactions with others; I found I had more patience during challenging conversations and could better empathize with my partner's perspective, leading to more constructive discussions about shared responsibilities. Journaling also became a valuable tool for processing emotions and identifying stress triggers. Technology played a crucial role too—tools like shared calendars and task apps streamlined our household management. Yet, challenges remain. Adapting to new circumstances, such as career shifts and growing children's needs, requires ongoing effort and flexibility. But these lessons have not only improved my life but also strengthened my relationships and sense of self. I've learned that perfection isn't the goal—progress is.

Real-life stories have the power to inspire and illuminate. Hearing how others have tackled the mental load can provide both validation and practical insights. Consider Sarah and James, a dual-career couple whose lives felt like a constant juggle of deadlines, chores, and forgotten commitments. Their decision to implement a digital calendar system came after a particularly stressful week when they both forgot key work meetings and their child's soccer practice in the same day. Sitting down together, they brainstormed solutions to manage their chaotic schedules. They settled on syncing their digital calendars, setting shared reminders, and allocating specific responsibilities for recurring tasks. This collaborative decision not only reduced their stress but also gave them a tangible way to work as a team, transforming their chaotic days into more structured and manageable ones. By syncing their schedules, they could easily coordinate tasks like grocery shopping and kids' activities. The results were immediate: fewer missed deadlines, a clearer division of responsibilities, and a newfound sense of partnership. They described how their evenings transformed from chaotic multitasking to moments of connection, cooking dinner together without the stress of forgotten chores looming over them.

Another family, the Rodriguez clan, implemented a weekly check-in routine. During one session, they realized that their mornings were consistently chaotic, with everyone scrambling to get ready on time. Together, they decided to create a morning checklist and set earlier alarms to give themselves more time. This small adjustment significantly reduced stress and set a positive tone for the rest of the day, showing how their check-ins led to practical and impactful changes. Every Sunday evening, they sat together to discuss the week ahead, voicing concerns, sharing updates, and redistributing tasks as needed. At first, it felt awkward as they weren't used to discussing household responsibilities so openly, but over time, it became their favorite ritual. The structured check-ins helped them feel more connected and proactive rather than reactive, turning what once felt like a chore into a meaningful moment of teamwork and appreciation. These moments of connection not only improved communication but also strengthened their bond as a family. Over time, they even began incorporating gratitude into their check-ins, each family member sharing something they appreciated about another, fostering a spirit of unity and positivity.

Challenges along the way are inevitable. For instance, the Taylors had to overcome deep-seated traditional norms that placed most household duties on the wife. Through active listening and persistence, they gradually adopted the Fair Play method, equitably dividing responsibilities and fostering mutual respect. Initially, they faced pushback from extended family who questioned the new dynamics, but by maintaining open dialogue and focusing on their own household's needs, they found a sustainable balance. Such stories underscore the importance of persistence and collaboration, reminding us that change is possible and deeply rewarding.

Cultural influences shape how we perceive and manage the mental load. Take Priya and Arjun, a multicultural couple navigating expectations from both of their families. Early on, they faced pushback when Priya's family questioned Arjun's willingness to share household responsibilities, and Arjun's family expressed concern about deviating from traditional roles. To address this, they held a series of candid discussions with both families, explaining how their shared system aligned with their values and mutual respect. They also invited family members to observe their routine, demonstrating the harmony and efficiency it brought to their lives. Over time, these efforts helped bridge generational gaps, fostering understanding and acceptance. While Arjun's family leaned heavily on traditional gender roles, Priya's upbringing emphasized shared responsibilities. By openly discussing their values and drawing from both traditions, they created a system that worked for them, blending traditional rituals with modern efficiency. For instance, they combined Arjun's family's weekly prayer gatherings with Priya's system of chore rotations, creating a balance that respected both cultures.

Another example comes from the Garcia family, who integrated extended family into their household routines. Weekly communal dinners became opportunities to share tasks, like cooking and cleaning, making the workload feel lighter. These cultural rituals not only eased the mental load but also deepened family bonds.

The Garcia children learned early about the value of collaboration, as they participated in setting the table and helping with meal prep, fostering a sense of responsibility and connection.

Despite cultural differences, some lessons are universal. Empathy, communication, and adaptability transcend borders, reminding us that understanding and cooperation are at the heart of managing the mental load. Diverse approaches to problem-solving inspire creative solutions, proving that there's no one-size-fits-all strategy. Stories like these emphasize that the key is finding what resonates with your values and adapting strategies to fit your unique circumstances. Whether it's through structured check-ins, cultural traditions, or community support, the common thread is the importance of intentional collaboration. Success comes from recognizing each household's specific needs and continually adjusting strategies to create a balanced and sustainable approach to managing the mental load.

Managing the mental load is a learning process, and mistakes are part of the journey. One common misstep is underestimating the emotional impact of unseen labor. Couples often overlook how much energy goes into anticipating needs, whether it's remembering a child's favorite snack or planning family vacations. This unspoken effort can lead to resentment if left unacknowledged. My frustration boiled over when my husband failed to notice the effort I put into organizing my children's extracurricular activities and the burden that comes with researching activities, attending trials, organising payments, and getting children to and picking up from the practice. All this, multiplied by three to accommodate for our three children. Our breakthrough came when he started acknowledging these efforts during our weekly check-ins.

As children grow older, they too should be encouraged to contribute more to household tasks. I constantly remind my children that they don't live in a hotel—we are a family, and if they want to live in a nice, clean, and orderly house, they need to help maintain it. Otherwise, we risk raising a generation of children who lack responsibility, expect things to be done for them, and enter adulthood without basic life skills. Instilling these habits early fosters independence and ensures that everyone in the household shares the load. A shift in household dynamics can often be achieved by committing to regular discussions where concerns are voiced, and small wins are celebrated. These check-ins not only improve communication but also encourage all members of the household to adopt habits that foster openness and appreciation. A structured approach to sharing responsibilities creates a sense of relief and fairness, reinforcing collaboration and reducing stress. Those who implement equitable task-sharing systems often describe an increased sense of balance and mutual respect, leading to a more harmonious home environment.

Reflecting on these stories reveals valuable insights. Flexibility is key—what works today may need adjustment tomorrow. Dividing responsibilities equally may seem like the ideal solution, but different work schedules, life demands, and unforeseen circumstances can make rigid divisions unsustainable. Adjusting responsibilities to fit changing needs creates a more practical and effective balance. For instance, one approach involves assigning morning and evening routines based on availability rather than expecting a perfect 50-50 split. This adaptability not only eases stress but also reinforces the importance of shared responsibility.

Flexibility and communication are essential in maintaining balance, and recognizing progress—no matter how small—can boost motivation. Simple moments, like restocking household essentials without reminders or recognizing when someone takes on an extra task, build positive habits. Over time, these small acknowledgments create momentum, making long-term change more sustainable. Growth in managing the mental load is an ongoing process of learning, adjusting, and appreciating progress rather than aiming for perfection.

There's immense power in community. While past generations relied on close-knit neighborhoods and extended families for support, today's sense of community has largely shifted online. Support groups, online forums, and social networks—particularly local Facebook mum groups—have become the modern-day village, where parents swap tips, offer emotional support, and share insights on everything from meal planning to managing bedtime meltdowns. These digital communities have taken the place of the in-person help that families once depended on, providing real-time advice and solidarity.

However, this shift also highlights how our approach to raising families has changed. In the past, relatives often lived nearby and played a hands-on role in childcare and household duties. Grandparents, aunts, and older siblings would step in to help, easing the burden on parents. But as economic demands have pushed more women into the workforce and families have become more geographically dispersed, many parents find themselves navigating these responsibilities alone. The result is a more insular and individualized approach to family life, where the mental load can feel heavier than ever. Without built-in support systems, parents must be more intentional about seeking help and redistributing responsibilities within their households.

Building a supportive network isn't just about receiving help—it's about fostering connections that empower everyone involved. For centuries, communities have relied on shared responsibilities to lighten individual burdens, creating a sense of collective strength. When support is reciprocated, it reinforces the idea that no one is alone in managing the mental load. Knowing that you have a network to lean on provides a sense of security, making challenges feel more manageable. It builds confidence in your ability to juggle responsibilities, ensuring that even during difficult times, you have a safety net that won't let you fail. By sharing resources, celebrating successes, and learning from setbacks, communities remind us that we're not alone in our struggles. The collective wisdom of shared stories proves that together, we can navigate the challenges of the mental load with greater resilience and joy. From practical tips to emotional encouragement, these networks provide the tools and solidarity needed to thrive.

Chapter 9
Sustaining Long-Term Change

Sustaining progress in managing the mental load requires proactive strategies to prevent regression. Life's unexpected twists—such as career changes, family emergencies, or heightened stress—can disrupt even the most well-intentioned plans. Recognizing common regression triggers is the first step. These triggers can include major disruptions like moving to a new home, returning to the office after a period of remote work, or navigating health challenges. Even smaller shifts, such as seasonal schedule changes or unexpected travel, can lead to setbacks. If you find that the start of a new school year disrupts your morning routines, leading to missed tasks and rising tension, start by identifying these triggers early to allow for proactive adjustments, such as planning ahead for busy periods or building in extra flexibility to accommodate sudden changes. For instance, the loss of motivation or slipping back into old habits often occurs during particularly stressful periods. Acknowledge these triggers and prepare for them with contingency plans to maintain your momentum. For example, creating a shared document to outline possible challenges and pre-emptive solutions can be a practical way to stay prepared.

Creating systems for accountability can help keep efforts on track. Regular partner check-ins, where both individuals discuss what's working and what needs adjustment, are invaluable. Some couples find success in utilizing accountability partners or joining support groups, which provide external encouragement and fresh perspectives. For example, one family implemented a monthly review session where they revisited their task-sharing agreements, identifying small tweaks to keep their system running smoothly. Others have found value in using digital apps to track tasks and provide visual progress updates, making the process more engaging.

Reinforcing new habits takes time and consistency. Research suggests it takes an average of 66 days to form a new habit, though this can vary depending on the complexity of the behavior. During the initial phase, focusing on small, manageable steps can make the process less overwhelming. For example, starting with a single task, like maintaining a shared calendar, allows partners to build confidence before expanding to more comprehensive systems. Consistent reminders, like setting alarms or using visual prompts, can also help reinforce new habits during this critical period. Tools like habit-tracking apps can be effective for monitoring progress and providing visual reminders of success. Establishing routines that align with new behaviors—such as a shared morning checklist—can also anchor these habits. Additionally, integrating rewards for sticking to new habits, like enjoying a shared evening activity after completing tasks, reinforces positive behavior. Learning from setbacks is equally important. Rather than viewing them as failures, analyze what led to the regression and adapt strategies to avoid similar pitfalls in the future. Each setback is an opportunity to refine your approach and strengthen your resolve, reminding you that growth is rarely linear.

Celebrating progress is essential for maintaining motivation and reinforcing positive behaviors. Recognizing achievements, no matter how small, validates the effort invested and boosts morale. For example, celebrating the completion of a challenging task-sharing adjustment can create a sense of accomplishment and inspire continued effort. Acknowledging milestones isn't just about marking the end of a journey; it's about appreciating the steps taken along the way.

Creative ways to celebrate milestones include small personal rewards or joint activities. One family celebrated meeting their monthly goals by creating a themed scavenger hunt at home, where each clue highlighted a recent achievement. The activity not only added an element of fun but also allowed the family to reflect on their progress in an engaging way. One couple treated themselves to a weekend getaway after successfully implementing a new division of household duties for three months. Another family created a "wins jar," where each member added notes about achievements big and small, reviewing them together during family dinners. These celebrations foster a sense of togetherness and shared accomplishment. Some families have even adopted themed celebration nights, such as "Pizza and Progress Fridays," where they reflect on successes while enjoying a fun meal together. Incorporating celebrations into your routine ensures that recognition becomes a habit. Monthly reflection sessions, where partners or families acknowledge progress and express gratitude, can strengthen bonds. A shared achievement board, placed in a visible location, can serve as a daily reminder of collective progress. Encouraging a culture of appreciation within relationships—through regular expressions of gratitude and mutual recognition—helps sustain momentum and reinforces the value of collaboration. Over time, these practices cultivate an environment where effort and success are consistently celebrated.

Flexibility is key to sustaining long-term change. As life evolves, so too must your strategies for managing the mental load. Recognize when adjustments are needed, such as when schedules shift or new responsibilities arise. Embrace change as a natural part of growth, viewing it not as a setback but as an opportunity to enhance your system. For instance, when one family faced the arrival of a new baby, they revamped their task-sharing plan to accommodate the additional workload, demonstrating the importance of proactive adjustments.

Strategies for continuous improvement include regularly reviewing and revising task-sharing plans. For example, one couple conducted a review after realizing that their weekday routines were leaving them both exhausted. By discussing their individual challenges, they identified that meal preparation was disproportionately falling on one partner. Together, they decided to alternate cooking duties, with the non-cooking partner managing cleanup. This adjustment not only reduced stress but also gave them more time to relax together in the evenings, demonstrating how even small revisions can make a significant impact. Involving all household members in these reviews ensures that everyone's needs and perspectives are considered. Seeking feedback, whether through casual conversations or structured surveys, can provide valuable insights. For example, one family introduced a biannual feedback loop where each member shared suggestions for improvement, leading to innovative solutions like rotating chore assignments to prevent burnout. Families with older children have also found success in incorporating their input, ensuring that adjustments reflect everyone's contributions and capabilities.

Tools for adaptability, such as digital platforms for tracking changes, can streamline these processes. Shared calendars, collaborative apps, and progress trackers allow households to stay organized and responsive to new challenges. Developing a mindset for growth and change is equally important. View each adjustment as an opportunity to refine your approach, fostering curiosity and experimentation. This mindset ensures that you remain open to trying new methods, even when faced with uncertainty. For example, experimenting with different meal prep systems can transform a tedious chore into an efficient and enjoyable routine.

Sustaining change goes beyond the present—it's about building a legacy for future generations. Instilling values of equity and collaboration in children creates a foundation for balanced mental load management. This legacy begins with creating a supportive family culture where everyone feels valued and empowered. One family, for instance, implemented a weekly family council to discuss upcoming tasks, fostering a sense of inclusion and teamwork.

Teaching by example is one of the most powerful tools for legacy building. Demonstrating effective communication, empathy, and teamwork shows younger generations how to navigate shared responsibilities. Involving children in age-appropriate tasks—like setting the table or organizing toys—not only lightens the load but also teaches responsibility and the value of contributing to a team. Some families use chore charts with stickers or small rewards to encourage participation, making the process engaging for younger members.

Educational tools and resources can reinforce these lessons. Family meetings to discuss roles and responsibilities provide a platform for collaboration and learning. Storybooks and media that emphasize equity and teamwork can inspire children to embrace these values. For instance, one family used a storybook about a team of animals working together to overcome obstacles as a springboard for discussions about teamwork and fairness. Another household created a family vision board, visually outlining their shared goals and responsibilities, which became a daily reminder of their collective efforts.

Empowering future generations to become advocates for balanced mental load management requires fostering leadership qualities and critical thinking. For example, one family encouraged their oldest child to take the lead in planning a family picnic. The child was responsible for creating a checklist, delegating tasks to siblings, and ensuring everything was prepared on time. This experience not only built their organizational skills but also instilled a sense of pride and responsibility, demonstrating the value of leadership and teamwork in a supportive environment. Encourage children to take initiative in organizing tasks or solving problems, and involve them in community or school initiatives that emphasize equity and collaboration. These experiences help them develop the skills and mindset needed to promote these values in their own relationships and communities, ensuring the ripple effect of change continues to grow. By embedding these practices early, families set the stage for lasting, meaningful transformation.

Conclusion

As we come to the end of this journey, let's take a moment to reflect deeply on the themes and insights explored throughout this book. At its core, managing the mental load is about fostering equity, understanding, and connection within our relationships. This concept underpins the strategies discussed throughout the book, such as equitable task distribution, which ensures both partners feel valued, and open communication, which lays the foundation for addressing invisible responsibilities and emotional labor effectively. By integrating these approaches, relationships can move towards balance and mutual respect. It's about dismantling the invisible burdens that many carry silently, redistributing responsibilities, and embracing systems that promote fairness and collaboration. From the first steps of recognizing these unseen tasks to building strategies for long-term balance, we've uncovered actionable ways to create more harmonious households and partnerships built on mutual respect.

One of the most critical takeaways from this book is the transformative power of equitable task distribution. When responsibilities are shared fairly, it creates a ripple effect—both partners feel valued, supported, and empowered to contribute meaningfully to their shared lives. Equally vital is the role of open communication, which fosters honest discussions about needs, boundaries, and challenges. By addressing these conversations with empathy and intention, couples can tackle even the most sensitive topics with confidence and care. For instance, one couple struggling with financial disagreements found that empathetic listening transformed their discussions. By focusing on understanding each other's anxieties about money, they were able to shift the conversation from blame to collaboration, resulting in a shared budget plan that met both their needs and reduced tension in their relationship. Managing the mental load also requires attention to emotional and cognitive labor, emphasizing the significance of mindfulness, empathy, and mutual support in sustaining healthy relational dynamics.

The strategies outlined in this book are not just tools for better organization; they represent pathways to profound personal and relational growth. Vulnerability and empathy, in particular, offer opportunities for transformation that extend beyond logistics. By embracing these practices, readers can foster a deeper understanding of one another, cultivate resilience in the face of challenges, and strengthen their partnerships in meaningful ways. These approaches encourage a shift from merely surviving to thriving together. Thriving means moving beyond managing day-to-day responsibilities to actively creating joy and fulfillment in your shared life. It looks like finding time for shared hobbies, celebrating each other's successes, and maintaining an open dialogue about your aspirations as a couple. For instance, one couple found that dedicating one evening a week to discussing personal goals and shared dreams strengthened their connection and gave them a renewed sense of purpose in their partnership.

But the journey doesn't end here. This book is a starting point, a foundation for ongoing dialogue about the mental load. Regular check-ins, continuous communication, and a willingness to adapt will ensure that the progress made is not only maintained but also evolved to meet the changing demands of life. Relationships are dynamic, and the strategies shared here are designed to grow with you. I encourage you to revisit these conversations, refine your approaches, and celebrate the progress you make along the way.

Taking the first step is often the hardest, but it's also the most rewarding. The initial challenge often stems from the fear of change or uncertainty about where to begin. For example, one couple found it daunting to address their imbalanced household routines but decided to start with a simple task audit. By listing out daily responsibilities together, they quickly identified areas to share and streamline. This small yet impactful action set the stage for larger changes, reinforcing that even modest beginnings can lead to meaningful progress. I urge you to implement one or two strategies discussed in this book today. Whether it's setting up a shared calendar, conducting a task audit, or scheduling a weekly check-in, starting small can build momentum and lead to significant change over time. Remember, progress is not measured in leaps but in consistent, intentional steps forward. Each small action contributes to a larger transformation, creating a ripple effect that positively impacts your household and relationships.

You are not alone in this journey. Engaging with a broader community can provide encouragement, insights, and validation. Consider joining online forums, such as parenting or relationship-focused groups, participating in support groups for mental health or family dynamics, or attending local workshops on communication and household management. These spaces offer opportunities to share experiences, learn from others, and gain valuable insights tailored to managing the mental load effectively. Collective wisdom is a powerful tool; hearing others' stories can inspire new ideas, offer fresh perspectives, and remind us that the pursuit of balance and equity is a shared goal. By connecting with others, we amplify our efforts and foster a sense of solidarity in our journeys.

To those embarking on this path, I offer my deepest encouragement. The road may not always be smooth, and setbacks are inevitable, but the potential for positive change is immense. By prioritizing equity and connection, you are not only improving your daily life but also setting an example for future generations. Your efforts are creating a ripple effect that extends far beyond your immediate household, shaping a culture that values collaboration, shared responsibility, and mutual respect. This is how lasting change begins—through the choices we make and the actions we take every day.

This book's vision is to empower individuals and families to achieve balanced, equitable relationships and harmonious home lives. It's a vision rooted in the belief that when we work together with empathy and intention, we can transform not only our homes but also our communities. Together, we can create a world where the mental load is shared, respected, and understood—a world where balance and equity are not just ideals but lived realities.

Finally, I want to thank you for your commitment to this journey. Your dedication to improving your relationships and engaging with the concepts in this book is both inspiring and humbling. I encourage you to share your feedback, stories, and experiences, as they can contribute to the ongoing dialogue and future editions of this work. By sharing your journey, you inspire others and add to the collective wisdom that drives meaningful change. Thank you for taking this step toward a more balanced and fulfilling life, and for being part of a movement that values equity, understanding, and connection.

Household Audit: A Comprehensive Task List

This household audit provides a detailed breakdown of visible and **unseen** tasks that contribute to the mental load. Use this list as a tool to assess who currently handles each responsibility and to identify areas where tasks can be shared more equitably.

Daily Tasks

- Meal planning and preparation
- Packing lunches for work/school
- Cleaning up after meals
- Wiping down kitchen surfaces and tables
- Loading/unloading the dishwasher
- Sweeping/vacuuming high-traffic areas
- Tidying up shared spaces (living room, kitchen, bathroom)
- Managing morning and bedtime routines for children
- Feeding and caring for pets
- Sorting and responding to urgent emails/messages
- Managing laundry (sorting, washing, drying, folding, putting away)

Weekly Tasks

- Grocery shopping (planning, list-making, purchasing)
- Meal prep for the week
- Deep cleaning of kitchen/bathrooms

- Vacuuming and mopping floors
- Dusting furniture and surfaces
- Taking out the rubbish and recycling
- Lawn care/garden maintenance
- Organizing kids' school bags, uniforms, and supplies for the week
- Coordinating social activities or weekend plans
- Cleaning out the fridge and pantry
- Paying bills that aren't on autopay
- Washing bed sheets and towels
- Reviewing and updating the family calendar

Monthly/Seasonal Tasks

- Decluttering and organizing common spaces
- Checking expiry dates on pantry and medicine cabinet items
- Deep cleaning neglected areas (baseboards, under furniture, vents)
- Rotating seasonal clothing and storing out-of-season items
- Planning and booking medical/dental checkups
- Vehicle maintenance (oil changes, tire checks, car washes)
- Managing subscription services (cancelling, renewing, adjusting)
- Reviewing family budget and financial planning
- Shopping for upcoming birthdays/holidays/special events

- Updating emergency contacts and household documents
- Checking kids' school supplies and replacing as needed

Child-Related Tasks *(if applicable)*

- School drop-off and pick-up coordination
- Helping with homework/study planning
- Packing school lunches/snacks
- Managing after-school activities and sports schedules
- Organizing playdates and social activities
- Attending parent-teacher conferences
- Tracking school projects, permission slips, and deadlines
- Ensuring school uniforms and sports kits are clean and ready
- Teaching life skills (chores, budgeting, cooking, self-care)
- Managing screen time and enforcing household rules

Unseen and Mental Load Tasks *(The often unnoticed responsibilities that contribute to running a household seamlessly.)*

- Remembering family and friends' birthdays, anniversaries, and special events
- Planning holidays, travel, and accommodations
- Scheduling and attending medical/dental/vet appointments
- Tracking family members' emotional well-being and providing support

- Managing household inventory (knowing what needs replacing/restocking)
- Coordinating child-care or emergency backup plans
- Anticipating seasonal needs (buying winter coats, summer gear, school supplies)
- Keeping track of family traditions and holiday rituals
- Researching household purchases (appliances, tech, furniture)
- Following up on ongoing tasks (delayed repairs, pending returns, disputes)
- Managing family finances, budgeting, and long-term savings goals
- Handling unexpected issues (sick kids, last-minute schedule changes, household repairs)
- Being the primary point of contact for schools, doctors, childcare providers, and social events
- Ensuring everyone gets downtime/self-care while balancing the needs of the household

How to Use This List:

1. **Audit your household** – Mark which tasks you currently handle and which ones your partner or housemates take on.
2. **Highlight unseen tasks** – Acknowledge the invisible workload that contributes to the mental load.

3. **Discuss and redistribute** – Use this as a starting point for conversations about fairness and balance.

4. **Create a shared plan** – Use task-tracking apps, a family calendar, or weekly check-ins to ensure tasks are equitably divided and adjusted as needed.

5. **Review regularly** – Reassess responsibilities periodically, especially during major life changes (new job, new baby, moving homes, etc.).

This household audit is a **living document**—as needs and circumstances change, responsibilities should evolve too. The key to reducing the mental load is **visibility, recognition, and shared responsibility**.

www.ingramcontent.com/pod-product-compliance
Lightning Source LLC
Chambersburg PA
CBHW072221070526
44585CB00015B/1440